Becoming A Man, In A Tough Journey

Matthew B. Holland

ISBN: 978-1-95-163017-1

Dedication

Quote from me

"Never forget where you came from and where you are trying to go in life."

Acknowledgment

Before you go ahead and read this book, I want you all to be familiar with the people who helped me write this book. These people are my family and friends who helped me become the man I am today. They inspired me to tell my life's story to help others learn about the challenges in life. This book also talks about the challenges that I have faced and overcome with the help of my near and dear ones.

About the Author

My name is Matthew Holland, and I am from Delray Beach, Florida. Throughout my life, I have faced many challenges and have been surrounded by naysayers. Since I lived on the streets for most of my childhood, people told me that I would continue to live like a thug for the rest of my life. I had to prove those people wrong about me. I wanted to show them you can be whoever you want to be if you put your mind to it. This book, *"Becoming a Man is a Tough Journey,"* is to show people who are going through something in their life that they can be somebody in life the right way.

Preface

Challenges. Mere challenges. That is what life is about, and that is what sets our path in life. The truth is, we all are a make-up of what life throws at us. Everything that touches us while we journey across this life is what controls our life, choices, and decisions.

Sometimes, when situations are unfavorable, that is when we start to swim our way to survival, to have a totally different life. To be honest, we are just one step away from having the life that we desire. And this book is just about these many life struggles that have changed and shaped me as a person. It is about how one decision turned my life into something worthwhile.

If I have learned something from my life, it is that you can do and achieve anything possible if you put your mind to it. No matter how many difficulties you seem to have been surrounded by, it all depends on that one right decision you make. And then, your resilience and steadfastness in living up to that decision or life choice is what makes you successful at the end.

Contents

Page Left Blank Intentionally

Chapter 1
The Boy From Delray

In all honesty, I, Mathew Holland, could not imagine what life had in store for me in my colorful youth. My early days in Delray Beach, Florida, were filled with ups and downs. At one point, my friends and I were enjoying ourselves playing games on the sidewalk. On other occasions, I would get myself into all kinds of trouble. However, in each situation, I somehow managed to sustain myself and gained tremendous experience in the process.

These experiences worked wonders for me and my personal growth as they clearly showed my strong points along with my weaknesses. This knowledge aided me in attaining my ambitions in life and made me realize the actual importance of other people. This is because whenever my life was influenced by another individual, whether it be my friends or family members, I started adjusting myself and my overall perspective.

Even though my parents had a limited amount of resources, they managed to secure the needs and wants of five children along with themselves. This was the reason why I never aspired for anything beyond the reach or capacity of my parents. On the other hand, I shifted my focus toward the things that were available to me and kept myself entertained as much as possible - even if that meant causing a bit of a stir in the neighborhood. Being the middle child of the family, I always felt an invisible barrier between my siblings and me. My two older siblings, Whitney and David, were usually the ones that told us what to do, while my younger brothers, Anthony and Willie, viewed me as their leader. I was the third eldest among the group and was usually confused about my role in the family.

However, in light of Anthony and Willie's behavior, I would usually get the motivation needed to carry on and pursue my juvenile actions. As a result of their support, it did not feel as if I was committing any social error. From my perspective, I was doing everything perfectly normal and what was expected of me at that time. I did not pay much attention to the realities of existence. However, I was always aware of the fact that I needed to accomplish something substantial in life. This was part of the reason why I became a nuisance for my family. I never wished to be a burden for my family or people in general. On the contrary, I simply wanted to live my life according to my own means.

I never wanted anyone to interfere in my routines or day-to-day practices and direct me on how to live my life. Even if my parents tried to advise me on something, I would listen to them but adhere to only those things that interested me. This is why I developed quite a reputation for myself and my partners in crime. I would usually overstep my boundaries to know the real extent of my potential.

This innate competitiveness would appear in almost every activity that I performed at an early age. At one point, this urge went to such an extent that I started picking fights whenever I would lose in a particular game. However, I never let any fight prolong for extended periods of time. Whenever I received any disturbing news about my actions, I would apologize immediately and try to resolve the problem. Among the fondest memories of my early youth has to be none other than my companionship with Tevin, Ian,Tyrell, Davon, and David.

Everyone from our parents, all the way to the neighborhood, knew that our pack would be found playing in one precious spot, Block 48 Park. This place had become our retreat from the harsh cold realities of the world. This is because it offered us space where we could freely express ourselves without any restraints or limitations. We used to play all sorts of games in that park without the threat of our parents lying in the wake. In addition to this, the nearby residents of Block 48 were extremely supportive as they never forced us to stop our games or control our emotions upon a victory. There were numerous instances when we caused a lot of noise in the park, yet no resident or administrator would come and warn us to stop our activities.

I was so fascinated by the place that I had actually stayed around the corner from the park my parents move to this area after we move from the complex Delray state with my uncle Chris. It was fun being with my family again, and it would also definitely save us all the time and energy that we spend walking to the park. There were a couple of games that we enjoyed playing, which included football. Like every American youth, we picked up the passion for football at a relatively young age. We were obsessed with it to such an extent that it started to take a toll on our health. However, it still did not stop us from practicing it and developing it even further. Other than that, there was a game called 'bust em up.'

The older children in school would tell tales about this game and how difficult it was. However, upon practicing the game, we learned that it was possibly the most enjoyable thing available at that time. The rules of this game were pretty simple. The players had to bounce or throw the ball up in the air and make a desperate attempt to catch it. The person who catches the ball has to run for a touchdown; if he gets tackled, he has to throw the ball back up, but if he continues to score a touchdown, he has to keep running with the ball.

Throw'em up Bust'em up was perhaps the greatest escape from school or any other responsibility, and we tried our level best to prolong these wonderful hours as much as we could. I would often run around without my shoes, and my mother would warn me at every turn. One day, I stepped on a shard pierce of broken glass, which served as an everlasting reminder of my errors in life. From then on, I never took off my shoes and continued enjoying these days. However, like all good and bad things, our games had to come to an end, and we had to return to our families and pursue our day to day routines. Apart from enjoying these games, my siblings and I would often visit Aunt Cynthia's home, which was right next door to our house. Albeit her strict persona, we would manage to play a handful of indoor games. Her daughters, Tiffany and Sharquet, would become a full member of our group and follow in our footsteps. The most common game we played in her house was none other than 'hide and seek.' The rules were pretty simple.

You had to hide in the house so the person who was counting couldn't found you if that person found you it was your turn to count. This was a good hiding place for us to play. In fact, Aunt Cynthia's house was really fun. My siblings and I enjoyed these days as much as we could because we knew the minute we returned, we would be trapped in the endless cycle of life. These visits were the ideal experience for me. However, one underlying factor became a significant cause of grief for me, and the rest of my siblings. This factor was none other than the behavior of my older brother. David had become a nuisance for me, and the rest of my siblings as he would consistently make fun of us whenever he got in trouble with my daddy.

David was ready and willing to do anything to cause us trouble, even if it meant beating us up. I remember one time David did something that affected me and the others for years to come. On that day, however, David did something horrible; he started beating up my little brother Willie, and that's exactly when we jumped in to beat up David. Tiffany, Sharquet, Carvlin, and Whitney were watching us, and Tiffany ended up telling my dad about the incidence. He rushed outside to put an end to our fight, and scolded my brother David; after all, David should know it's what he deserved for always trying to find ways to bully us. After that, I ushered into a new era of bliss as my pack found another great instrument of enjoyment: the PlayStation. A majority of my childhood revolved around playing the PlayStation 2. There was an attraction to the console that could not be explained to an average person.

However, if you ask the people who played it, they would describe it as a perfect blend of knowledge, entertainment, and critical thinking. The experience was surreal, to say the least, and it greatly helped me understand the world from a different perspective. Tyrell, the brains behind our group, would agree with me in this assumption, as he was the one who always knew everything about it. We were never really the same after playing the PlayStation. Apart from the PlayStation, we also developed new ingenious ways to keep ourselves entertained.

Although I had numerous friends in my youth and practically everyone knew me from the neighborhood, I felt comfortable only when I was surrounded by my pack, which consisted of Tevin, Tyrell,

Davon, Ian, and David. Tyrell, however, was a different story altogether. He managed to divide his intellect in such a systematic form that he found ways to keep himself entertained, excel in his academics, and also provide well for his family. This was a unique ability and found mostly in a handful of people in this material plane. I learned a lot from his life examples, and it was because of him that our group survived even the direst of circumstances. Even if we somehow got ourselves into trouble, he would never be in it. He was driven to succeed and overcome all obstacles. Given that, I also found some way to continue my existence and persevere. Like in the case of all groups, there had to be someone who gets in trouble the most. In our case, it was none other than David.

He would find some way to endanger himself, and we had to fight people because he could not control himself. He would always get into trouble for the wrong reasons. But at the end of the day, he always sustained his position as a close friend. He was like a brother, and we knew each other since we were little more than four years old. We tolerated his indecent action for a while. However, when things became really bad, I started running the streets. As a result of my actions, I found myself in jail, and also suffered from an injury that resulted in a total of 5 stitches; I got bitten by the police dog.

To be honest, it was one of the hardest decisions I had to take, but it was one of those things that needed to be done. I could not continue my life in a violent and unstable way because that was not the way I was brought up by my parents. Because my parents wouldn't want me in the street, I could not see any form of justice happening for me. This is why I had to let go of the street and focus on building a career and a secure life.

The next couple of years were extremely difficult for me because I had lost one of the most treasured people in my life, my dad. My father and I were very close, and he served as my trusted confidant throughout his time in this material plane. This is why a couple of months following his death, I became suicidal. My mother and the rest of the pack knocked much sense into me following the event, and from then on, I approached life in a lighthearted manner.

Part 2

One of the strongest bonds on earth is shared between the members of a family. It takes more than just a mother, a father, and a child to build a family. It takes love, understanding, tolerance, patience, and a small hint of pain and resilience to make a family. There are many people in this world who we consider a member of our family despite not being related by blood. It takes a family to turn a house into a home.

Family is not only built by blood, but it is also a combination of trust and support. The foundation of a family lies in hopes of each other. The people within a family share emotions that are far more beautiful than any other emotional bond. The concept of family has now grown outdated in some places on earth, but it remains to be one of the strongest foundations in the world. No force on this earth can break a family apart unless the power is handed to an outsider who is looking in.Family can be the strongest team on the earth and also the most fragile bunch at the same time. All it takes is miscommunication and misunderstanding to break family ties. Everyone, at some point in life, has a falling out with a member of a family, but these fallouts can always be repaired by talking out. As I said, I felt both cursed and blessed as a child who grew up with siblings.

My siblings, especially my older brother, gave me a hard time. But they were also the people I made one of the fondest memories with in my life. I miss all the fighting and crying that took place, all the troubles I got in, and got my siblings in. Out of everyone in my family, my sister was the go-to person for me. I would go and talk to her about everything I could not mention to my mother.

We shared our secrets and came to each other for help when need be. Childhood was the most precious time of my life. I believe that everyone in this world would agree to that. Everyone missed the time when they had no responsibility on their shoulders. At the time, they did not carry the burdens they were carrying both on their shoulders and hearts now. Things have tremendously changed. People have walked down the wrong path once in their life only to be brought to the right path. Other unlucky few remain stranded on the wrong path for the longest period of time.

Chapter 2
Siblings

Siblings play a big role in our lives. Not only are we raised side by side with them, but we are also forced to share everything with them. They help us shape into who we are today by either advising us or making us go through various experiences. They are a constant in our lives-or, so we like to think. But siblings toughen us up and back us up when we need them the most.

It does not matter how much you fight with your siblings; at the end of the day, they are the only people who are going to be there for you. I admit that my siblings were also there for me when I needed them the most. But then again, they also teased me to the point that I wanted to fight.

Well, I wish I could say that the time I spent with my siblings were all good. There were some good times and bad times, but mostly bad times since me and my siblings always fought and struggled. I don't really know where I stood with my siblings at that time. One can say that I share a certain love-hate relationship with my siblings. Things might be better now comparatively, but it does not mean that I can easily forget what happened with me during my childhood. Even after years, I still cannot get over the incidents that happened between my siblings and me. It might seem minor incidents to others, but for me, it shook my entire world upside down. As you can see, we all struggle with something. That means that my siblings and I were always at the end of the receiving stick. Some days we would go without food, and sometimes water, and lights would get turned off. I used to see my mom cry, trying to see how she was going to pay the bills; however, my mom always found a way as she always prayed and asked God for help. God always found a way to do right at the right time.

My eldest sister and brother always had each other's support; meanwhile, my youngest two shared their secrets with each other. My bonding with my siblings was strong. My eldest sister, Whitney, was the person I talked to about everything; David was the one that I fought with all the time. In fact, he would push to fight him, but at the end day, we always hug. Anthony, who was born after me, was always the quiet one; he was the one I always used to play the game with. Then there was the youngest one, Willie, who was spoiled rotten. Willie was the naughtiest one out of the bunch and always got away with everything. Most of the time, my parents would either be too focused on the elder ones or too busy pampering the younger ones.

They say that the middle child is the forgotten child, and in my case, that was actually the case. It was the course of nature that led me to be the forgotten one. As the middle sibling, I feel my mom expected the most out of David, the second eldest. Anthony and Willie were always fighting David. My mother always passed it off as 'boys being boys' and never did anything to stop it. Of course, she would punish us from time to time whenever we crossed the line, but it was never enough to stop David from bothering us, until one day. I remember the time when David got into big trouble in school, and my dad tried to take the role of punishing him. He dragged David out of the house to lawn mown people. Dad had him around the blades and loud noises from the lawn services as punishment. It was the highlight of my day since I knew how much David hated the lawn mown people. It was quite sunny, and the weather was hot.

I was staring at him through the window and laughing at him. I couldn't help myself; it was a funny sight to see. David crying and scared, and knowing that it was his punishment, made it more humiliating for him. I kept laughing at him until he noticed me laughing at the window glass. At that moment, I knew I was a dead man. David came inside and yelled at me at the top of his lungs to stop me from laughing at him. I could only scream back at him as he tried to stir more trouble. My dad, who thought that David would get better after being on punishment, noticed that he was creating more ruckus.

As a result, I thought I would be punished, as well. It was an unfair punishment, but as I said, as a middle child, I was always at the receiving end no matter what. I hadn't done anything to him, and yet I was scared of being punished. How was that supposed to be fair?

Luckily, my dad did not punish me like I was anticipating, and he went to sit somewhere else.

"HAH!" I shouted in David's face and ran away.

What can I say? I was pretty naughty too. It was quite fun to anger David as well. He had no choice but to accept his defeat and go back to his punishment begrudgingly. David was the second eldest brother, and as a result, he always thought he was the boss of things. It sucked being his younger brother half of the time. He would take over the game and would break it if we didn't let him play first.

Willie was a taker, and his habit got worse with the passage of time. He didn't care what he was doing unless he had what he wanted. It was one of the reasons why Willie had grown up to believe that everything my siblings and I owned was his. He was forgetting the core values of morality, one after the other, and no amount of punishments were going to straighten him out.

My siblings and I were getting tired of Willie's attitude, as well. There was no point in hiding our things from him if he was going to create a ruckus and take it anyway. No amount of hiding our things helped us out in our favor. In fact, it always backfired because Willie would find them and take things from my mom as well. I don't know whether Willie really loved us at that point. His constant fights at one point made me hate him, and I even hated the fact that we were brothers.

Since David was not planning to stop beating up his little brothers any time soon, we came up with an idea to get him off our back. This one time, I was sitting on the tree, and David was mad about something. He started yelling and messing around, and I warned that I would punish him; he didn't stop. I was trying to punish him when Willie and Anthony jumped in, and we jumped on David.

We gave David the beating of his life. It was not fair how he always got to hit us around, but we could never do the same. There were some things that David can only understand through fists, and it was his bad attitude that led us to hit him in the first place. David was a big boy compared to the three of us. It was a challenge to take such a big boy down when we were all so young, but at the end of the day, we had finally beaten David to a bloody pulp. I don't think anyone of us thought that what we were doing was wrong. We were all kids, and not to mention, we were all boys excluding Whitney.

It was bound to be a madhouse with that many boys in one house. Whitney lived in her own world because, firstly, she was the eldest, and David could not mess with her. Two, she was our sister and being a girl eliminated any chances of her being messed with, and she knew how to fight as well. She was really close to me, and she and David used to fight each other all the time. However, David never bothered troubling Whitney as much as he was fighting with me, Willie, and Anthony. I believe that we drove our parents to the point of insanity, sometimes with all the fighting that took place. But it was always David picking on us and not the other way around. Something about it was different this time since the tables had turned. It was finally us versus David, and we walked out as victors. It was a big deal for boys at that time to finally stand up for themselves. I don't think I ever felt more manly in my life than when I finally stood up to my brother David. It is not easy to stand up to my brother David, and it was definitely not easy to stand up to him; he was always bigger than me.

As I said, siblings can be a total pain in the neck, but they love each other at the end of the day. We, us brothers, used to fight a lot, especially when we went to live with our grandma; we used to fight so hard that we put holes in the wall and our grandma used to curse us out and tell my daddy about our mischief; my daddy would come with his belt, and I used to be the first one to run. I did not like getting a whooping; my dad was a big muscular man, so when he hit us with that belt, it really did hurt my brothers and me.

Of course, you, as an outsider, would tell us to toughen up. You would not know about the pain until you walk in my shoes and live my life from my point of view. Willingness did not matter to David, but I think we taught him a lesson or two after ganging up on him together. The childhood I lived in was not all that bad. My siblings and I would tease each other from time to time. We would give each other stupid challenges that would make us cry with laughter. There were more than fist-fights taking place within the household. There was joy, as well. As siblings, we made each other do stupid and senseless things. Whitney, my eldest sister, could not help but be a part of all the ruckus that took place in the house. She had once challenged my younger brothers and me to roam around the neighborhood wearing her undergarments. She even told us that she would give us a hundred dollars if we did it. I was not the one to shy away from such challenges, especially when money was involved.

Hundred dollars was a lot for people like us. So I wore her undergarments and roamed around the entire neighborhood. I might have become the laughing stock for that day. All the kids in the neighborhood guffawed as I walked past them, but I didn't care. I was more concerned about winning the challenge and making a hundred bucks. I could buy anything with a hundred bucks, no questions asked. I could buy new games for my PlayStation 2 or new toy cars.

We came from a middle-class family and were not so well off, so it meant a lot for me to get my hands on that money. That day later came to an end when my father found out that I was walking around the neighborhood wearing Whitney's undergarments. He was furious beyond belief that I did something that stupid. It might have seemed fun to my sister and me, but it was a big deal for my dad. He scolded me and screamed his head off. At that time, I did not understand why he was getting so angry at me. We were just playing around and having fun. Dad was thinking more from an adult's point of view and how much I was giving him a bad 'rep' in the neighborhood. To be very honest, I had a very complicated childhood. Some days would be better than others, but I remember the bad days the most. Like every other human out there, I easily forget about the good days when I come across the bad ones. I do not know whether that was a good thing or a bad thing. Either way, at the end of the day, I was either fighting with my siblings or having fun around with them every once in a while. I think that is what makes the bond between siblings so special. You hate them half of the time, but then you also make precious memories together.

I got a cousin named Robert. He was Sharquest and Tiffany's older brother and was the cousin that always was fresh everywhere he went. He told me I used to watch Westing as a little kid. Westing was a tv show about cowboys that were always fighting with each other and shooting each other. People call it the Wild West, and I used to watch it with my grandma all the time. My cousin Robert told me I would cry and want to fight whenever someone would change the channel.

Part 2

The human psyche is quite fragile. The smallest of shocks and setbacks can damage it forever. My life had been a series of troubles and misfortunes. While I'll forever be grateful to the friends and family that had always been there for me, they could do nothing for my fragile mental health. The deaths of close ones changed me. Parents have a direct influence on their children's lives, and a father becomes a role model for the sons to look up to, and the daughters to know what to look for in a man. The duty of the mother lies in nurturing the child, while the father has to show the right direction to their children with their life choices. Every step taken by the parents is noted by a child, no matter how young that child may be. Some things remain in the back of our minds. My father was one of the central figures in my life.

No matter how tough and rough he treated his kids, he still loved us dearly. None of us doubt that even for a second. Everything he did was for his children. Every time he punished us for getting out of control, we did not know at the time that it was for our betterment and nothing else. But as I grew up, I realized many things that I would not have as a child. He wanted to see his boys grow up into fine young men, but could not see any of us reach manhood in his life.

Perhaps that is how it was meant to be, but I pushed through it. There was a time in my childhood where I absolutely loved dogs. They are one of the most loyal creatures on earth who would protect their owners till their last breath. A dog is more than just a pet for some. He is a man's companion, and I had two dogs throughout my life who were my companion as I walked down the harsh journey to become a man. My dogs were more than just pets for me. They were the closest friends I ever had in my life after my cousins and siblings. Dogs are majestic creatures, one of the most significant parts of my life. Most of my childhood memories comprise of DC and Rock. Rock was my first ever pet. He got hit by a car, and watching him die had left a deep scar within me. Rock had died after getting hit by a car. The best part of coming home from school every day was seeing Rock because I always knew that he was waiting for me to come back home. He was a beautiful dog who loved to tackle people whenever they came home. He would hug me, and I would play around with him. We would play so many games together, and I spent the majority of my time with Rock. He was the best pet anyone could have asked for, and I always thought he was more of a friend than a pet.

One day, I came home, all excited from school to meet Rock. I was always eager to meet him, and so was he; he would eagerly wait for me to come home. As children, we make everything seem more significant than it really is. The feeling of anticipation and excitement lingered in the back of my mind as I tried to find a way out of the school bus.

Watching him being buried in the backyard after getting off the school bus was the first most painful thing I had ever seen. I lost a part of me when Rock passed away as he was my very first pet. Losing a pet is one of the worst things that could ever happen to a person. Most people keep pets for therapeutic purposes, and it has been scientifically proven that people who own pets are the happiest people on earth. I thought I was happy until I lost Rock. The loss was still bearable, but it got worse when I lost my second pet named DC. He was a pit bull, and I had immediately formed a strong bond with him. He did not remind me of Rock and had an entirely different personality. He was one of my beloved pets, and I cherished him like I had cherished Rock. DC was a fantastic pet, but he met his demise as well. A part of me swells in guilt because DC died after eating dog food and roach poison after it. He was a happy pet, and I could not get over his death. I thought he could help me get over Rock's death, but just like people, even pets are irreplaceable. Death always came around for the people and animals I loved.

After losing both DC and Rock, I am no longer the biggest fan of dogs or just any pet. Pets are supposed to heal what's broken in us, but the demise of my pets ended up breaking me further. They were a part of my family, and I just couldn't think about getting another one and losing it too. Most people who see their pet-owning friends cry over the death of their pets probably believe that they are overreacting. However, they do not know that they are not just pets. You spend every waking, walking, and breathing moment with your pets the moment you adopt or buy them. They have feelings and can show emotions, as well. A unique form of responsibility falls on your shoulder as soon as you adopt or buy a pet. They can detect your feelings and try to console you when you are down. Pets are unique companions, and they all hold a special place in our hearts. No words can describe their love.

However, after coming to terms with my losses, I can no longer stand pets anymore. I didn't want a dog in a while because they remind me of the pets I had in the past. That is why I believe that the human psyche is one of the most fragile aspects of being human because it takes one moment to ruin your perfect memory into something that leaves a bitter taste in your mouth. I know what roles psychology plays in this, but it is still a little strange to accept the reason I didn't have dogs in years. Whatever the reason is for not having a pet anymore, I knew that DC and Rock had to be a part of this book. They were my best friends, and probably the only companions who entered my life to spread happiness around and left nothing but sadness behind.

Rock was my first pet, and sadly DC will probably be the last pet I would ever own. There will always be a part of me that will drown in guilt for not taking care of my pets. But that is just life, and I did not want to add more individuals on the list that would soon leave me. Not because I was afraid of losing them. I was scared of becoming attached to them because it gets worse when someone leaves after you are so emotionally attached to them. One could say I had attachment problems, but then again, we all have obstacles in this life.

I do not want to create another obstacle that will prevent me from becoming the best in this life.

Chapter 3
Delray State Complex

Making friends was one of the many things that we could effortlessly do when we were kids. We did not care how our friendships and relationships would benefit us; it was just about having as much fun as possible. This world seemed a lot more colorful when we were kids. There was no such thing as responsibility, and we couldn't really care less for consequences at that age. I remember how I spent most of my time playing around and wreaking havoc around the neighborhood with my siblings.

Life only becomes grey and white when we grow up and learn the word known as 'responsibility.' There are times when I look back at my childhood and envy my younger self, who had nothing to worry about in this world. I never had to be burdened with the bills and expenses. My only concerns were limited to the playtime while I left the responsibility up to my parents.

As a kid, I understood the importance of making friends. Friendship was a relationship that connected virtual strangers to each other, and tied a special bond between them, making them members of the family. Moving to Delray States Complex was not easy to deal with.

I moved into uncle Chris's house, along with my elder brother David, and my sister Whitney. My two younger brothers, Anthony and Willie, were staying back with my dad and my mom. They were living with my aunt Cynthia. This had caused a rift between us siblings. Leaving our parents did have some effect on us, but we did not know what was going on. I was just a kid who was clueless about what was going on, so I passed my time fooling around like many. I remember the day I made one of the most amazing friends in my life.

David and I were sitting at the stairway because we had nothing better to do. We were still new to the complex, and we had no idea what to do since we did not know anybody. It took us some time to settle down to the new place since the change of environment affected us immensely. Everything seemed so strange here. These two boys, named Chris and Bryan, approached us and offered us cookies. We accepted the offer and hit it off right away. That was just the beginning of our innocent friendship as we started hanging out more and more. Bryan and Chris were both brothers, as well. Bryan became my best friend, and Chris became David's best friend.

We formed a childish rivalry and often got into trouble with each other. Bryan was a good kid, and we always played around at the complex. He had a dog who liked to bite, so I used to play with his dog even though I would be scared of being bitten. Bryan had a pleasant personality, and we shared a lot of things in common. Our friendship flourished over time. One of the most memorable things about moving to the Delray State was the lake situated near it. My uncle Chris always warned us to not go to the lake, but we were curious children who were hell-bent on moving from one adventure to another. Sneaking off to the lake was one of the many exciting adventures we walked into, mainly because kids like doing things they are told not to do. My best friend and I would sneak off to the lake anyway.

It was an average lake, and there was nothing special about it, but still, we enjoyed spending our time there. We would go fishing in the lake. There was a time when Bryan and I spotted something akin to big turtle swimming in the lake. We did not know what it was at that time, but now that I think about it, the creature we saw in the lake resembled a turtle. We had been fascinated by the sight because we had never seen one of those in real life. Anytime my Uncle Chris found out about us sneaking off into the lake, he would give us a whooping. Bryan and I did more than just rebel against my uncle's wishes. We would spend our time fighting with David and Chris, or we would play football with each other.

We stirred a lot of trouble even when we played with each other. Not a day would go by where we did not get into trouble. It was as if trouble was our middle name. It was a sunny day, and Bryan decided to play football. I had agreed to play with him because I could never turn down the offer of playing football. We played with David and

Chris as well, and it was one of the very few times when none of us thought about starting mischief. However, our honest intentions did nothing to save us from trouble because I was soon being scolded for breaking someone's window. We were playing football, and I had thrown a ball so far that it ended up hitting and breaking someone's window. For some reason, I found that the entire situation was quite hilarious. It was one of the most hysterical moments of my life because, for once, I was not going out of my way to seek trouble.

But trouble had found its way to me, and I ended up causing problems for someone unknowingly. I was a kid at that time, so there really weren't any paybacks or repercussions, and I was quickly let go after a good scolding. Delray State Complex was a nice place with a safe and welcoming environment. We were allowed to play outside as often as we wanted, so Bryan and I spent many afternoons playing football together as well. He was my go-to person whenever I wanted to play some game. He was into athletics as much as me, and that was one of the many reasons why we grew closer. The entire year at the complex had been fun thanks to the friend I made along the way.

This experience helped me realize the importance of friendship from a very young age. The saddest thing about growing up is the resulting loss in your sense of creativity. I had surely lost mine as I transitioned from childhood into the pre-pubescent years. As children, we tend to overlook the problems right in front of us. A child's innocence is quite enviable because they can ignore everything that is going around them. My life seemed pretty comfortable at the time. I had nothing to worry about, and I could do whatever I wanted. This world seemed like a vast place, and I was not afraid to explore it at that age. I had no idea what I wanted, but I knew that whatever I did would be taken care of because I was young.

However, we all come across one moment in our life that wakes us up from our dream-like state, forcing unpleasant reality upon us. Our sweet dreams are shattered as we grow up, but mine gradually went downhill after I lost my father. That night when my dad passed away, I was throwing rocks with my friend, breaking car windows; every car that passed, I threw a rock at it. Next thing you know, I heard my phone ring. It was my sister calling, and she was crying hard on the phone. I asked her what was wrong, and then she broke the heart-wrenching news. Daddy was dead. I ran so fast like I was the 40-yard dash for football.

I couldn't believe it at all. I could see everybody crying all around my house. I walked to this park called 7th ave park to clear my mind. This was the park I used to go to all the time to smoke my blacks to make myself feel better after crying. It was a loss that could never be restored; no matter how many times I tried to recover it. I had lost my father to death. Life had gotten the best of me, and the moment I lost him made me realize that I was never going back to be the same kid again. Experiences tend to tone down our happiness bit by bit, and that was the turning point in my childhood that made me realize that things could never go back to the way they used to be.

Losing my father felt like I had lost a part of my childhood, and that is something that would always affect me, even as a grown-up. I could never get over it, no matter what, and that was just the beginning of my downhill journey.

Chapter 4
Death In The Family

Death is one of the most feared concepts in the world. Every one of us in this world knows that death is inevitable, yet we all fear it when it comes knocking on our front door. People who proclaim that they aren't afraid of death, do not realize that the joke is on them. It is bound to happen to each of us, and accepting it will not make it any easier when it comes.

Life and death share a strange relationship with each other. When life is born, death comes along with it. When we come into this world through the entire birthing process, we bring death with us into the world. Life begins with the first heartbeat, and so does death. Once there is a possibility of being alive, there will always be the possibility of dying. As a child, I never really worried about death.

When we are young, the only thing we care about is having fun and making the most out of this life. Childhood comes with the blanket of naivety that prevents us from seeing the real horrors of this world. We learn about the world and its horrors, first at home. We only know good from bad if our parents have taught us about it. In life, we all must have wondered the reason behind such laws. Curiosity peaks at the tender age of ten. It's when a child realizes their mind and thoughts. Why are my parents telling me to stay away from strangers? What is the reason? Instead of following orders, they wonder about things. We marvel at the way things work in the world. No amount of schooling and guidance can teach us about life and death the way real-life experience does. I witnessed death when I was in 8th grade. An unfortunate heart attack had taken away my father when I was just a boy. His death affected me immensely. Growing up, a boy needs his father the most. He was my guiding compass, and without him, I was lost.

As a result of this loss, I began acting out. I rebelled against everything because my mind could not comprehend that my father was no longer here to guide me. Sure, he scolded me a lot, but that was only because I placed myself in dangerous situations willingly. I would rather hear him scold me every day than not have him here with me, and the pain of it all made my personality change entirely. That was the first time when I understood the concept of death, and how every one of us has to go through the entire process of living and dying.

However, just because I understood the cause of my open wounds, it did not make things easier for me. I couldn't handle life anymore. I did not realize that losing loved ones to death would become a common occurrence in my life as I grew up. The thought of it scared me out of my mind. But true to form, life gave me another blow. He was more than just a cousin and a best friend; he was like a brother, and then he vanished from my life.

It had taken me a lot of time to adjust to reality after losing them. But time heals all wounds. I had gotten better and thought I was on the verge of being okay again. My life was looking good. Well, as good as it can get. I was in Village Academy, one of the many stars on the football team. I had gone through the lows to reach the top. When you go through so much to reach the top, you believe that no one can bring you down when you are on top of your world. I was entering the prime years of my life and trying to turn it around. That did not mean that others were in the same position as I was.

My cousin, Davon, and I were pretty close. He has always been a part of my heart, and I considered him one of my brothers. Davon and I were closer in age, and we shared many fond memories of our childhood together. We grew side by side as his birthday was in April, and mine was on the 15th of March. We were raised together and shared our bond of family that goes back to the diaper days. Davon was the one person who supported me the most when my father passed away. Davon was a single child, and he had no sisters or brothers, which contributed to his closeness with all of us.

He stayed over at our place so much that one might think he was one of my siblings. He blended with us all so smoothly. I never thought I would lose him so early in my life, and the thought was so far from reality. Davon met his demise in the worst ways possible. The night he died was the night I went on a date with an ex-girlfriend. I had asked her out after contemplating for many days, and I was happy to score a movie date with the girl I liked while I was at Village Academy. I was a young boy, and having the first date meant a lot to me. It was supposed to be a typical night where I went on a date and would later come home happy with how things had progressed there.

I would be a total charmer and a gentleman to the girl I had invited for the night out. I was thinking this when I left the house to go on a date. I had bought the tickets to my favorite show, and the girl I was on a date with also liked the movie I had picked out. We got settled down in the cinema theater, and I was excited to reach the point where I would hold her hands. I had my hopes up and even thought about giving her a kiss at the end of the date. The movie started, and I was expecting romance. After a while, out of nowhere, my phone rang. It rang for a while, and I finally picked up only to hear the words leave my mother's mouth. *"Willie and Davon got shot! Willie and Davon got shot!"*

She was hysterical, and I could tell right away that my mother was crying. The words rushed out of her mouth in hysteria. She then repeated her words again, and this time she progressed from her first sentence. *"They shot 'em! Davon is dead!"* The person on the call could say nothing further than that, and I immediately got up and made my way out of the movie theater.My mind was racing with a thousand thoughts all at once. What? How? When? Where? These thoughts were running through my mind as I tried to make sense out of the situation.

I had seen Davon right before I left. How can they be dead within a few hours? The thoughts swirled around my mind until I could comprehend nothing anymore. I tried to apologize to my date while she was trying to calm me down. Her mom ended up giving me a ride back home as I anxiously sat in the backseat. As soon as her mom pulled over to our house, I immediately jumped out of the car and saw people crowding around my house. I was just astounded to see the police cars with their red and blue lights blinking. All I could see was the yellow tape and people surrounding the area.

The yellow tapes meshed with the red and blue lights, a combination of which gave me a headache. The entire process was surreal, and to this day, I cannot remember much of it. My body was on autopilot, and my mind had gone silent. I could no longer hear the cries of my mother and sister, or the people talking in hushed whispers. I still come up blank when I try to remember the event. There were so many people I had to walk through that I did not know if I would reach Davon right on time.

Davon's body laid there, covered in a body bag, with his blood splattered all over my garage. I tried to make sense of the situation.

What were Davon and Willie doing here in the front yard of my house? They were planning on going to the dance at pompay park in the city, so how did it come to this? I couldn't understand anything. I tried going inside, but the police officer stopped me and told me, *"You cannot go back inside. We're looking for somebody."* He did not elaborate, and his word was law.

My front yard had just become a crime scene, but that was not what fazed me out of my mind.

Davon was dead.

I could not digest the news at the moment. I was numb to everything. You know when you go through something shocking, your brain shuts itself down to protect itself. My brain had shut down until my mind was just filled with white silence. I wanted to know what happened. Why was Davon dead?

All I wanted at the moment was information on how everything happened. One of the police officers there for the investigation of the crime scene later informed me of what went down. Davon and Willie were on their way home from the dance when a guy pulled up in the front yard when they were just getting there. The stranger knew Davon, and they fought over something.

To this day, I will never know what the fight was about. But the guy followed them to the front yard. My mom tried to stop the fight before it could turn ugly, but she was too late. The guy who was fighting with Davon pulled out a gun and shot Davon and Willie. The guy shot Davon five times. He shot Davon three times on the mouth, and two times in the stomach. Willie got shot two times in the groin area, and he had thankfully survived through it all as he ran for his life. Willie knew that the man was trying to kill both of them. Davon, on the other hand, was trying to get on the bike so he could get home. Who knew he would end up falling dead before he could take off? He loved us all, and a part of me believes they would have killed my brother if they could. Willie was only thirteen, and he barely made it through. But we were all thankful that he had survived. Davon was seventeen, and he was no longer here with us. The family was shocked.

None of us could process what had happened. We lost a brother and a son. He had his whole life ahead of him, and it was taken from him with such cruelty. None of us could fathom his pain during his last moments. My mom and sister had witnessed everything, and they were still reeling from the traumatic event they had just seen. Davon was around my age and having someone die at the same age as you can really mess a person up. I was trying to make sense out of this situation.

I tried to think, *"Why did this happen? Why did it come to this? I'm trying to do well. I'm trying to do the right things in every aspect of my life. Why does this have to happen? Why do I have to go through the pain of losing another loved one? Why did it have to be him?"* I was grateful that Willie had survived, but he will carry that scar with him for the rest of his life. He would be traumatized for the rest of his life, and the rest of us would be severely scarred forever. Davon was our brother. We shared almost everything together. He often talked about his future ambitions. Davon told me about what he wanted to be. He shared his dreams with me and told me he wanted to be a professional football player one day. I was sitting there beside him and said, *"Oh, you can do it."* I would encourage him to pursue his dreams, no matter how hopeless our situations seemed. Like I said, no one in my family had ever even gotten close to graduating High School. At one point, I also believed that I would drop out of High School, but here I was, still trying to complete High School. I was too shocked by the death, but it was harder for Davon's parents.

Davon's parents were more than devastated because Davon was their only child. Being the only child, he was pampered and loved immensely. He was their only hope, and now they did not have him there with them anymore. The situation was bitter, and the reality was harsh. But Davon would never be with us anymore, no matter how much we wished he was here with us. I did not know how to cope with this situation. Death had already become such a scary prospect in my mind. I thought nothing in this life would be as painful as losing my father, but here I was, wrong again.

The death impacted me, but I did not dare to stray off my path. I had seen how it would end up, and I did not want to end up in a place as scary as a juvenile center. Being unbothered about something as big as this is impossible. All of this had happened on the weekend, and I wondered if I should go to school or stay at home. My family was all over the news by then already, and I did not know whether I was ready to go back to face everyone. *"Should I go to school, or leave it alone?"* I thought to myself, and after doing a lot of thinking, I dragged myself out of bed. A part of me felt lifeless as I got ready for school. The routine was so monotonous that I'm not sure if I even knew what I was doing. But I somehow reached school and immediately regretted it. Everybody in the school came up and asked me how I was doing.

They would say, *"Are you okay? I saw the news and found out what happened."* Or *"I saw that your cousin got killed. Are you sure you're okay?"* They were not taunting me either. They were trying to welcome me warmly, but I could not grasp the reality of the situation just yet. I was so confused about everything and was still reeling from the fact that Davon was dead.

Everyone was coming up with the best interests, but their warmth was just a constant reminder of how cold I was feeling deep within my soul at the news. Their kindness was a continuous reminder that Devone was dead. It was a constant reminder of that night, a night I wished to forget and wanted to accept all the same. When you go through something like this, it takes a long while to accept the situation and reality.

All I can think is, *"Why? Why is this happening? I'm trying to be good, and I'm trying to do good for my mother and sister. I'm trying so hard to turn my life around. Why is this happening?"*

The continuous loop of 'why me' was going through my mind. Why did it have to be me? As if losing my father was not bad enough, I lived through another loss. The entire situation was absurd and unfair. I had been in a long slump after my father passed away, but I knew that he was in a better place now. I tried to hold on to the end of the rope, no matter how hard it got for me. I tried to be kind to everyone, but a part of me wished that they would not talk to me.

I wanted them to pretend I did not exist. It gets worse when everyone knows what you went through. People look at you like they understand what you are going through, but they only see the surface. None of them knew what was hiding underneath and what I had gone through to improve my life after losing my father. How was I going to do that after Davon's death? It really messed me up for a while. I knew the impact would be long-lasting.

His death hurt me really badly.

After dodging questions and sympathetic condolences as nicely as I could, I walked down the school hallways, when the principal of the school approached me.

He said, *"Matthew, I saw what happened on the news. Are you going to get them back for what they did to your cousin?"* I looked up at my principal and told him that I want to be somebody in life. I want to make my cousin Davon proud of me. The principal smiled, the kindest smile ever, and said, *"You, young man, are strong."* And that was it. That was our conversation. He just wanted to know what I would do now. No matter how much I loved Davon, I knew getting back at those boys would end up being fruitless. Either way, I would end up losing the life I had tried so hard to build for myself. I was not ready to give that up. I was driven to complete High School for both his sake and mine. His death helped me realize that I still had the opportunities to accomplish my dreams and goals in life. I was grateful for the life I had and upset with the life that Davon could have had.

No one would ever know what he was capable of becoming in his adulthood. He was no longer there with me. We would never get the chance to exchange our dreams and hopes for the future together. I would never get the opportunity to meet him up again or spend time with him again. I would never see him smile, except in my memories. Sadly, death is an everlasting concept and will forever be a part of my life until the day I die. Understanding this bit does not make me feel better.

Despite knowing how it is bound to happen, death can never be easier for anyone. Hearing about someone's death always stuns us to our core. The thought of people being here one day and gone the next day immensely scared me. I could no longer run away from the truth nor hide from it. The death of my father stunned me first, and I had acted out because I was young. But I knew better, even if I was as young as seventeen, I knew enough not to repeat the same mistakes in my life. There was no such thing as second chances, and this was a painful period of my life. My experiences taught me better, and I knew what to do now. There was no way I could afford to stray off this path I had laid down for myself. There was a time when I was not in control of my life and choices because I did not know better.

But I know more than I did before. My experiences made me wiser. Trying to keep my life together was not an act that conveyed that Davon's death was any less saddening than my father's. It meant that I was a better version of myself now and knew that everything in this life hinges on one decision. It takes one choice to make our life, or break it. I had to decide carefully about what I wanted to do now, and that is what I did.

The thought hurt me, and it was painful to live on like this, but I lived on. Not just for my sake, but also for his sake. I knew I had to live on to achieve my dreams, and that's exactly what I did.

I lived on.

Chapter 5
Trouble

It is tough being a trouble-maker in a world that is continuously striving for perfection. People hate those who stir troubles in their way and do their best to avoid them. However, most people were attracted to me because I always got myself in a sticky situation. Like most boys out there in this world, I always got into one trouble after another.There was so much energy bursting inside my body that I took it out by running around and creating havoc wherever I went.

Children get into trouble every once in a while, but it always seemed as if trouble would find its way around me. There was so much that I wanted to do. This might have given my parents a little tough time to deal with me, but I bet that it was the troubles that they remembered the most. My sister always said that I loved to follow her around. I was the type of person who would easily get attached to people. So, I guess I got attached to my sister, Whitney, even before I learned how to walk.

We would always joke about how I started following her around as soon as I learned how to walk. She always recalled that time and told me that I once hit her in the head with a pot when I was one-year-old. It was because she was trying to fit into my brother David's boxer shorts, and I guess I did not like that. I did not like it when she would take her attention off of me.

I wanted to keep Whitney all to myself since I loved her so much. We did grow up and went through the same phases as many other kids. Whitney would always threaten me to blurt out my secrets when she wanted me to do something for her, *"I'm gonna tell Mama if you don't do this, Mattie."*

And I would always stand there before her with a sassy expression and say, *"I don't give a damn about what you wanna say to Mama, Whitney. I'm gonna tell her what you did."*

And we would follow each other with empty threats that now seem quite silly and hilarious. This was only the beginning of my life as a naughty kid. I had many more troubling encounters in the coming years of my life. I indulged myself in many mischievous endeavors, which make me realize how troublesome I was. There were always times where I would come out of these accidents completely unscratched, and with all my limbs surprisingly attached; I use the word 'surprisingly' here because I had been a wild kid. Then there were times where I would have multiple bruises. I was sure of one thing, and it was that there were no in-between when it came to stirring troubles in my life.

My family would tolerate all these troubles, but there were other times I would get punished for it. There was not a day that would go by without stirring up one sort of accident or another. Most of the time, I would be the one hurting myself. I was not exactly hostile. I like to think that these troubles did not stem from violence or anything. It originated from just being naughty and nothing more. I always craved for some excitement in my life and wanted to distract myself. I liked the adrenaline rush that I would get whenever I did something I was not supposed to do. There were many instances where I got into trouble with other people besides my family. I was mischievous and always did things I was told not to do.

Perhaps I did not like listening to others, despite the discipline I would receive from my parents. My dad was mostly strict sometimes and soon became immune to whatever dilemmas I would stir up. There were many instances where my endeavors would land me into hospitals. One of the scariest experiences of my life was going through an allergic reaction at the age of ten. I was playing outside with my friend Tevin and noticed a bush of berries.

Those berries just drew me in, and I found myself eating one or two. That is how far I was able to go with eating these berries before I had trouble with itching. I did not pay much mind and ate another one before I started seeing bumps all over my body. My friend Tevin's step daddy noticed that there was something wrong with me when I started scratching all over my body. My body was full of bumps. I do not remember much as I blacked out. All I remembered was the ambulance taking me to the hospital. My mom thought it was one of my other brothers that was in the hospital until they rushed there to find it was me. My mom asked me why I ate those berries off the tree; honestly, I didn't know what to tell her. I didn't think anything would happen to me. All I wanted was to try them. But thankfully, after they gave me a shot in my butt, I was fine. I remember a teacher named Mr.Bernadette from Caver middle school; I used to get into trouble with him all the time. I also remember a friend named amp; he was the class clown and used to ask me to hit the song for the class. The song was called 'yes dude,' and I would start beating on the desk, and he would start dancing on the table like we got a music video going on; the whole class would start laughing, but the person that was not laughing was Mr. Bernadette; he gave me and amp detention. I had really turned into a bad kid.

There was a lady named Mrs.Ginny. She was the dog pound lady, and I used to see her every day. I used to go there to see new dogs every day. She was a lovely middle-aged woman who was always friendly to me. There was a gate I had to pass through to reach her office; it was called City of Delray animal control, and being a mischievous kid, I found out the code of the gate and tried to open it using buttons; it was fun to see things like gates open by themselves, and so I ended up going with my cousin Davon one day and told him the code. He inserted the *code and tried to warn me to watch out for the gate as it started opening.* But nope, I never really was the kind of kid who would listen to others. I always did whatever I wanted because I was naughty. I did not listen to him and directly jumped off the gate. It was almost a practiced move, and I was confident enough that I would not hurt myself. I was later proven how destructive my confidence was.

I was completely misguided by my confidence in overcoming any obstacle that came my way. I ended up spitting my fingers wide open when I was about to jump off the gate. I had screamed and ran all the way home while crying all the way there. My Mama saw me, and she immediately started fretting over the wound.

My Dad just told me, *"Put a band-aid on it."* My dad did not say that to be mean. He only said that because he was tired of me going out seeking trouble. Even after I told him that I could see the white meat of my bones through the cut, he only said to my mother to go wash up my wound in the bathroom. I was bleeding everywhere, and the pain was agonizing. All I could do was scream and cry at the top of my lungs. The house became more chaotic.

Mama said, *"I'm going to take my son to the hospital."*

Mama was always protective of us. Therefore, she rushed me to the hospital after wrapping my bloody fingers with a cloth. We reached the hospital, which was becoming a frequent scenery in my childhood, and I ended up getting stitches. Mama kept scolding me the entire way, *"I told you not to play on that gate, Matthew. I told you not to do it. Now, look what you've done to yourself."*

She was angry, but I could see that she was also upset with the entire incident. There were around six stitches, to be exact. We went back home after getting my hand stitched up, and all my family was outside when I got home asking me if I was ok. Then after I had healed, I went back to the hospital to take care of the stitches that needed to be taking out, and I even lost the function in one of my fingers. But, thankfully, only one finger turned out to be hurt from the accident.

It was somewhat reasonable to know that after going through such a horrifying experience, I only managed to mess up one of the fingers. I thought I was going to lose my entire hand. The gate had cut me open so deeply that I could see through the inner side of my flesh. I had torn the muscles in my hand and could even see the bones. It was somewhat terrifying, but also relieving to know that I could have lost so much more if my mother had not taken me to the hospital when she did.

These major troubles always led me up to the hospital. I always thought that many other kids like me visited the hospital after stirring up problems, but so far, I had not come across many kids like that. Few of these kids ended up endangering themselves like I did, but not that frequently.

Then there were minor troubles I would get into for doing stupid things. I would end up accidentally hurting my brothers because of it. My dad once took me and my brothers, David and Anthony, to the gas station. We were all excited, and like always, I ended up throwing big rocks around. One of the rocks that I threw ended up hitting my brother Anthony in the head, and it bruised him badly. I honestly felt bad because of it, and I got into trouble with my dad. I told him we were throwing rocks in the puddle, and what happened to Anthony was merely an accident. But my dad was furious, and so I ended up getting a whooping so bad I couldn't even sit down at all.

I had a close friend named Tyrell, who was like a close brother to me. He did not have a fatherly figure while growing up, and my Dad was the closest thing he had to it. He respected and loved my Dad like the rest of my siblings did. We would always have fun whenever he came for a sleepover. Pillow-fighting was the tamest thing we would do to have fun.

Tyrell was a fantastic friend who stayed by my side through thick and thin in life. He did not mind whenever I would get into a situation that would bring trouble or punishment for me. He was a great friend that always had my back no matter what. These experiences were quite scary, and it made me wonder how I even got out of them alive. From running around to eating berries, to cutting my hand open, I was still standing alive here to this day. These experiences proved to be trials for me later in life. I was taught one lesson after another whenever I got into these troubles. Every setback had a lesson hidden behind it, and I understood the hidden lessons one by one as I moved on in my life. I would have never known I was allergic to berries if I had not eaten those berries that day. The reaction could have been much worse later in life if it had gone undiscovered later in my life. Nearly breaking all of my fingers knocked some sense into me to never go over the gate ever again.

I would not have learned all of these lessons if they were not taught to me the hard way. Being hot-headed also made me learn a lot of lessons. And there were too many fights to count. At first, I thought that the world had something against me. I always ended up getting the short end of the stick and would place my blame on my surroundings.

But I knew better now and took complete responsibility for whatever I did in this life. I was always fearless and tried to climb trees in my spare time. Something was fascinating about climbing such heights. Soon, a person entered into my life and realized my potential. I always stood up for myself and needed some outlet to let it all out even after joining several sports in school, such as football, baseball, and soccer now and then. Soccer was hard to play, but I never gave up on it. I kept on pushing myself to figure out how it worked. I remember rejoicing the day I got the hang of how to play soccer. I remember playing for Village Academy high school; it was my first game, and everybody was looking at me and making funny of me. I didn't care.

Learning how to play soccer helped me understand that I was a young man who enjoyed challenges. For a long time, I always thought that challenges were hard to achieve because I feel like I couldn't do it. But now I understand why I did whatever I did. I was a sucker for challenges and enjoyed figuring out how to win them. Later on, my coach helped me realize that I was not attracted to trouble. He helped me understand that I was attracted to adventures and challenges. He guided me down the road of self-discovery, and I could not be more thankful to him for it.

Chapter 6
The Wake-up Call

Life has the strangest way of jolting us awake from the pleasant dream of ignorance. I was just a normal kid, maybe a little naughtier than other boys my age. Everything seemed simple. The naivety of my childhood had been that blissful dream, and the wake-up call was nothing short of antagonizing. I came face-to-face with one harsh reality after another, which made me realize that this world was big and bad.

The world is safe and limited for a normal kid who doesn't experience it until they become a teenager. As children, we hold on to people around us like lifelines just to make ourselves feel safe. However, the wake-up call is lurking around for all of us; we may not know it yet, but it will startle us when we least expect it to. Then we'll know what this world looks like in reality.

For me, the shock came in the form of my father's death.

I was only in 8th grade and around 14 years old when my father suffered a heart attack. He passed away abruptly, and that loss took a significant toll on my family. He was the head of the family, the rock that kept us grounded. We had our fights, but he was my father and my guardian. Losing him was akin to losing the anchor that keeps the ship at bay.

Yes, he was exceptionally strict with us, but I later understood the reason behind his harshness. He wanted to prepare us for the world so we could face its trials and tribulations with our heads held high. He understood very well that it would eat us up if we went out into the world unprepared. However, now that he was gone, who was going to show us the way, and stop us from walking down the wrong path? My mother locked herself in the room. She didn't want to face the world anymore. Her grief over losing her love was so profound that we ceased to exist for her.

We were her children, her flesh and blood, but her heart was broken. She tried to be a mother, but it just wasn't in her control anymore. She was often too out of her senses to notice that I was sneaking out of the house. I did not know how to deal with the pain of losing a father. The trouble was that I had lost my mom along with him. As kids, we place our parents on a high pedestal because we think that they know how to do everything in life. We believe that they will always be there for us no matter what. Losing him made me question everything in life.

It hurt me to know that he was no longer here with us. I was angry and in pain, and I did not know where to direct that rage. My mother was grieving in her way, and she was too far gone to care about me.

So, I ventured into the real world as it stretched out its claws to hook me in. In hindsight, I can tell that I did not understand what I was doing. I got into the wrong crowd just because I had nobody holding me back anymore. I hung out with the older guys because they were cool. They smoked, drank, and 'hung out.' They carried guns and ran around in the neighborhood. It seemed like a good life. They had everything I wanted for myself. It was also an exhilarating experience for a 14-year-old kid who had been exposed to so many things at a very young age. Before I even knew it, I was slowly sinking under the surface. I mimicked these guys at every chance I would get. I mirrored the way they would smoke until I smoked regularly. I walked with a confident 'swagger' just like they taught me. I carried a real gun around just because I could, and no one stopped me. I eventually ran away from home. My mother had finally started waking up from her slumber of grief, but it was too late by then. I had packed my bags and left the house several days before she noticed.

I was a child of the streets now.

My mother called me a few days later and begged me to come back home. She cried her eyes out, but I was addicted to this life. I was stuck with the decision I made for myself. My mother accepted my fate and settled into her new life. I spent my days spreading mischief with my new friends. We'd loiter around all day long, harass the passersby, and pretend to be men when we are barely even boys. This lifestyle wasn't sustainable, and we needed money to survive on the streets.

It started small. We'd rob the local shops and pickpockets to get by. Of course, this wasn't enough for boys who were hell-bent on destroying themselves. One day I joined the gang as they were robbing a woman. We scared and threatened her with guns to the point that she would have given us the clothes off her back. We took her phone, wallet, and watch. Just as we had thought we had executed a successful night time robbery, the sirens started blaring behind us. The police had caught us red-handed.

My friends and I got caught, and I got bitten by the police dog. I had been arrested at the age of 14. Ironically enough, it was April's Fool Day, and life played a prank by bringing me face to face with the consequences of my reckless actions. I felt the hard steel digging into my wrists as police officers pushed me into the car with brute force.

They put me in a wheelchair after I got bitten by the police dog, and then I ended up getting stitches. They drove me to the police station after that. It turns out that despite my terrorizing ways, I was still a kid. My heart was pounding hard as the police car drove me to the police station. I was old enough to know that I had gotten myself into some serious trouble. I didn't want to spend the rest of my life locked up for my stupidity. I didn't mean to hurt anyone. The police called my mom to tell her about my arrest. She thought that my older guy 'friends' were pulling a prank on her, and she cut the call. That confirmed my worst suspicions; no one was coming to save me.

They sent me to the Juvenile Detention Center since I was too young to be in jail. However, it still didn't mean anything because I still ended up going to the county jail. Other kids in the detention center were worse than hardened criminals; they looked strange. Maybe they were trying to gauge if I was capable of daylight robbery. Did I really have it in me to rob a grown woman of her belongings and wave a gun in her face? After all, your crime defines your worth in the detention center. No one cares what family you come from, and how you are as a person.

I got to taste that life behind bars as a robber.

But I couldn't last for more than a few days. I called my mom one day, crying and begging her to get me out of the Juvenile Center. I was sick to my core. I didn't want to be treated like a criminal anymore, even though I knew I deserved it. My mom only told me, *"That's what you get for not listening to me and disobeying me. Find your own way out of there."* She cut the call. She wanted me to own up to what I had done. I know she was ashamed of me and who I had become.

However, I couldn't help but reminisce about the boy who had needed his mother. I had only wanted to be held and told that we'd survive without my father. Then life showed me one of the harshest realities of this world. It taught me that every action has a consequence. I spent months in that center, thinking about what I had done. I questioned, day after day, if this was the life I wanted for myself. I asked myself, *"What do I want to do with my life? Do I want to repeat and do the same thing I'm doing right now? Or do I want to become somebody?"* I had an obvious choice. I had tasted the life of a criminal at a very young age, and now I was living the results of that. The trouble was that I didn't know if I could even move on with my life at this point. I had been an accomplice to a crime that did not seem that big a deal when we were planning it. For the longest period of my life, I blamed the circumstances that put me there that day. But that's the thing about living with the consequences of your actions. You can keep blaming everything else, and everyone else but yourself, but eventually you have to come around and face the truth. Every step I took that day, every decision I made that day had led me into that situation.

I had no one else to blame but myself.

Now I had to rise above my situation and make sure I never end up in this position again. I started working towards my betterment. I called my mom one day and told her I would get better. I was determined to start my life all over again. I was done running away from home. I understood that I could not run away from things for the rest of my life. I was ready to face my consequences, and that I would walk out of the center as a good boy.

"I want to save my life," I said to her. *"I want to get better."*

The silence at the other end bothered me a little, but I waited. I had made my mother's life hell; I should have been there to hug her when dad died. So what she couldn't look after me in those days? She was still my mother, and I owed her this much. *"I'm so glad to hear you say that,"* she replied finally. I could hear the relief and happiness in her voice. This was the first time in a long time we had a mother-son conversation.

I finally put the phone down. I knew the only way to go now, was up. I had to get better. I'd promised my mom that I'd make her proud. Unbeknownst to me, my mom went to court every day on my behalf. My coach, Robert, also went with her often. I had let so many people down. Here they were, doing their best to get me out of the Juvenile Center.

Three months later, I walked out of the court. I was a free kid, but I wasted no time. I got into school and put all my energies into passing eighth grade. My mom had made it very clear to me that the only thing she expected of me was good grades, and I wasn't planning on letting her down.

I worked hard to get into Village Academy High School. It was like crossing a milestone in my life. Running away from home, then getting into crimes, being surrounded by bad influences showed me what life would be like if I chose to walk down that path again. I wanted to become something at that point. I wanted to become somebody. However, there was still a mean streak left in me.

I wanted things my way, or I didn't want them at all. So I started slipping up thinking a drink here or a black mild there wouldn't hurt me… and mom didn't have to know. Just like that, I started skipping classes. I would hang out with the guys and smoke. I told myself that this was not as bad as getting in with the wrong crowd, but I forgot to tell myself that I wasn't supposed to be doing this.

I missed half of the school freshman year, and after the first two semesters, I ended up getting a 0.4 GPA. It was hard for me to see what I had done to myself again. My mom didn't know because we didn't have a house phone. But she somehow found out that I was missing the school and bunking lessons. The first thing she did was to sit down and talk to me. After my father had passed away, my mother got more into talking with us. She no longer liked to 'whoop' us the way she did when we were kids. She treated us like adults, even though I acted childishly at times.

I told her I wasn't ready for school because of my GPA in the first two semesters.

She only looked at me and asked me, *"What do you want to do then?"*

I honestly had no idea. I couldn't possibly drop out of high school. She told me that everyone in our family doubted I'd be able to do it because I was into ESE. The work was hard for me, and she knew it.

Thankfully, one of my old coaches was there to help me, as well. He said, *"I don't want you to be in this school anymore. You should come to the village academy."*

I took him up on his offer and discussed this opportunity with my mother. She agreed, but I had another obstacle to overcome now. I had to take summer classes because my GPA was so low. I had to pass the summer classes to get transferred. I took four classes in three months and worked hard for good grades. I knew I wanted to have a better life. Somehow, with the help of my coach and family, that 0.4 GPA turned into a 2.0 GPA. It might not be much for other kids, but for me, it was everything. I couldn't help but be proud of what I had achieved in three months. It had seemed impossible at one point, but right now, it was in the palm of my hands. I second-guessed myself often while studying, but the hard work and dedication paid off.

My life became a series of wake-up calls after my father's death. The first wake-up call was the one I got when I surrounded myself with the wrong crowd. They became my role models, and I became their puppet as I mimicked every single thing they did. I was fascinated with the streets, surrounded by booze and parties; it was a fantasy life for any kid my age. I enjoyed it because I got to experiment with them without having a care in this world. Every wrong seemed right until my life shoved the consequences of my choices in my face.

My world turned upside down, and I came face to face with the second wake-up call in my life. I was thrown into a juvenile center and isolated from the world. I was locked up for committing a crime that had only seemed like child's play. However, later on, after getting out, I worked hard to improve my grades to become somebody. I have talked about these things earlier.

Now, you must be wondering, what was the next wake-up call? Well, it was the realization that everything in this life is attainable if you believe in yourself. A person needs to push themselves past their limits to get ahead in this life. No one is going to hand you what you want. You are supposed to choose your goal and then earn it.

This world was not going to stop for me. It would go on with or without me. I had to make sure I became worthy enough to be remembered with honor. My last wake-up call was all about realizing that if I worked hard enough to achieve something, it would eventually come to me.

Turning my GPA over was difficult for me. Any student out there can testify how hard it is to raise a GPA from scratch. But I did it because I had put my mind into it. As a result of my hard work, I finally ended up getting into Village Academy.

Chapter 7
The Man That Changed My Life

I have always been a fighter. As a kid who always got into trouble, it was easy for me to get into one feud after another. The fighting came naturally to me since it was the only way to survive in the neighborhood. Many kids in this world avoid fighting because they know that the trouble that comes with fighting is not worth it. But I had accepted quite early on that I was not going to be like those other kids.

Despite my small physical appearance at that time, I always got into fights with other kids because it was an outlet for my energy. Most of it was harmless quarreling that had no real consequences at that time. I did not exactly enjoy these confrontations, but I always knew that trouble would find me, so I had to be prepared. Kids fight all the time, but we always took it up to a notch.

For me, it was more than just about self-defense; it was about survival. I was walking down the path to self-destruction like every other kid around me. Coach Rob guided me towards the right path and helped me understand that there was more to life than getting into trouble. Coach Rob taught me lessons and supported me through thick and thin. Coach Rob was the one who stopped me from fighting.

Whenever a fight took place, everyone could hear the excited yelling and hooting in the entire area Kids would always encourage other kids to fight harder, and I fought harder during such animated street fights. One day we were at Block 48 Park with Coach Rob. He would bring out the boxer gloves. Tevin cousin knocked me out with one punch; I thought I was tough. He was also my little lead coach. He coached us with a stern expression, telling us to keep going and never to give up. There was something about his demeanor that said that he meant business; he made me a better football player. I was playing for this team called Delray Rocks. I remember he had shown up in my life in 2002, and years later, I figured out that meeting him was quite possibly the greatest event of my life.

He had given us his boxing gloves and instructed us to fight like two players getting ready for a boxing match. I remember how cool Coach Rob was that day when he had separated us and told us to fight properly with rules. He had shown up out of nowhere and interfered with our street fight even though there were many other kids around us. None of them had tried to stop the fight. However, for some unbeknownst reason, Coach Rob had decided to step in. He had taken the lead, and that was something I would never forget. Coach Rob had taken me under his wing after he had noticed my talent on the football field.

In his words, I was better than my brothers, who had bigger physical builts. He chose me only because I always gave my hundred percent whenever it came to football fighting whatever it was. I did not enjoy fighting because I didn't like hurting others. Like any other kid, it was just another source to keep ourselves entertained. After spending time with Coach Rob, I discovered that he was a High School student who took on training as a boxer after school hours. He played football as well. He taught me all the tricks that I needed to know to defend myself. He took me under his wing and helped me exercise my aggression in an appropriate manner. Robert had noticed that I had too much energy that was just waiting to burst out of me. He taught me to channel it in more productive ways. He had grown to be more than just a football coach. Sometimes I believe, he was like an older brother for me. He looked after me and made sure to teach me about life even though I was not his responsibility.

The way he catered to my needs made me feel as if he had taken me on as one of his duties. That was one of the greatest gifts he could have given me. Watching football games with him became a part of our daily routines. He had discovered my love for football and always kept pushing me towards the sport. I used to play football as a kid, and Coach Rob knew about it. He got selected for his High School's football team, and my admiration for him grew tenfold. Robert always pushed me to work harder, academically, as well. He had noticed that I was not an outstanding student. I always got below-average grades, but then again, grades were hardly a concern for me. I was a kid, and kids loved to play around and have fun.

We never truly think about what to do with our life when we are young. Naturally, the future was not a concern for me. All I cared about was living in the moment, and Robert knew that. He did try his best, and I would always give him credit for that. He pushed me to focus on my education, but I was a reckless kid. Grades were hardly on top of my list of priorities. I do not think that I even had a priority list, to begin with. Now I realize how important it is to have a mentor in your life. Coach Rob had played the role of my mentor and older brother, guiding me towards the right path.

What he did for me was so much more than just a kind gesture. He looked after me even though no one had asked him to do it. He took me under his wing when no one had instructed him to. He was there for me during the darkest times of my life and helped me become a better person. Coach Rob had encouraged me to believe in myself even when I thought my life was falling in shambles.

There was just something fascinating about the way he had easily become a guide and my best friend at the same time. Coach Rob was a true source of inspiration for me. And then he had to leave, as he went on to pursue a college degree later on. Life has a weird way to knock us down when we least expect it. That's what happened to me when I could feel myself falling down a spiral hole. Robert had done his best to rescue me from myself, but his best was not cutting it for me. I had nothing but my stubbornness to blame for that. My life had taken a complete turn, and things had become difficult for me, and I could no longer cope. There was so much going on at the same time, and he was there to witness my lows. My admiration for Coach Rob only kept increasing. The lessons he taught me would always remain safe with me. He always saw me in a different light. He saw a part of me that I did not know existed, to begin with. He was the driving force behind my urge to change my life. Coach Rob's existence had made a significant impact on my life, and for that, I will be forever grateful.

The role he played in my life motivates me to become the driving force for other kids who think that it is impossible to turn their lives around. I made one mistake after another and still made it out perfectly fine. These mistakes came with a price, and the only reason why I was able to move past my mistakes was that I was able to learn from my mistakes. It is quite natural to make mistakes in our lives, and we cannot simply walk on eggshells around it.

It is inevitable not to make mistakes. Everyone makes mistakes, but the most important part of it is learning from it. If we keep on repeating the same mistakes, then we will come across a point where it is impossible to make amends. I made one mistake after another in my life, but Robert had always been there for me. He did not mind my mistakes and only encouraged me to learn from them, and honestly, it was his belief and support, along with my family's that made me into the person I am today.

My transition from a troublesome boy to a sensible man was certainly not easy, and meeting my coach was only the beginning of my walk down the road to becoming a man, and it was a tough journey. Coach Rob accepted my mistakes, even when I could not bring myself to accept them. My life may have taught me how to survive while I was walking down my tough journey, but it is true that I was only able to move forward because of the support I received from everyone around me. This is one of the many reasons why I wanted to help other kids who are like me. I want them to know that as long as we hold onto that one person who sees the light in us, we can reach tremendous heights in our life.

My childhood was not exactly a bad one. I grew up in a loving family and a loving environment; however, it is easy to become a victim of the streets. We all come across our weak points, and losing someone dear to me was my weakest point. However, before that, I had gone on to live one adventure after another.

Chapter 8
Village Academy

I sensed that I desperately needed a change in the environment. I did not know this, but I was certain I should be around people who understand me. Everyone in my old school knew me well. They knew that I had failed my courses and hung out with the wrong people. They avoided me like the plague because no one wanted to be seen with a failure. It was depressing, and coach Rob knew that I could never excel in such an environment. Coach Rob knew that I needed someone who could relate to me on a level that would ease me.

Getting into the Village Academy was one of my first achievements. It was the first thing I did for myself that proved to be healthy for me. There was a spark inside me, and the happiness of reaching one of my goals is something I cannot forget to this day. When you work hard and give it your all, the result is worthy. We give up on ourselves halfway through because we keep doubting ourselves.

We tell ourselves that we are not worthy of the goals we have set for ourselves, and just like everyone else, I had fallen into the same pattern. I told myself that I could not do it. At the back of my mind, I told myself that I would never make it. Raising your GPA from the ground and studying the same courses all over again was not an easy feat. After going through countless failures in my life, I had given up on myself academically. All I could think about was how dumb I was. Thinking about this every day messed me up. I came close to giving up countless times. I cried myself to sleep, wondering if the results would be worth all the pain I was going through.

Then came the part where I would swallow myself in regret. *"If only I had studied beforehand."* Or *"If only I had steered clear of the wrong people who distracted me."* Regrets are human emotions, and it is something we cannot push out of our system just by telling ourselves to get over it. Regrets clung onto me like a second skin, and it would hurt me from inside out. There even came the point where I thought the school was not important, and that studying was useless for me. What was I going to after studying? I did not even have a clear career in my mind.

I was lost and unsure of what I wanted to do. No one asked me what I wanted to be when I grow up. As I said, no one in my family even passed High School. I came from a family of dropouts and was close to following their footsteps. I always told myself, *"If they can't do it, how can I?"* I would compare myself to everyone in my family and tell myself that I was not unique. I thought that I would follow into their footsteps and become just another member of the family who could not make it to high school. It was easy for me to do this, as well. No one would judge me for dropping out.

I was more inclined towards enjoying my life to the fullest by involving myself with the wrong peers. It was the only thing I knew how to do. These dark thoughts would consume me and distract me from studying. Sitting there before my open textbooks, I would ask myself, *"What's the point? I can't do this."* But then I would remember the time I struggled back in the Juvenile Center and remembered how I felt when I was in there.

I would remember the feeling of being trapped because of how they monitored me for every second I spent there. I would recall all the times I cried and sobbed to my mother, begging her to get me out of there. I did not enjoy being there one bit. The food, the people, everything back in Juvenile mocked me. Then I would remember the promises I made to my mother. My mother had faith in me after I came back from the Juvenile Dentation center. She truly believed in me, and I did not want to disappoint her again. It was the last thing I wanted to do because I had done my fair share of disappointing her throughout my life. I had told her I wanted to be the one to save my life. I had told her I wanted to get better.

Was I so incapable of improving myself academically? Sure, it was a challenge most of the time. But like every challenge in this world, it was a challenge I could get over and come out with a winning card in my hand. My coach had faith in me, too, and it was their faith that I needed the most to push myself past my limits. I studied, and I made sure I studied hard. I wanted to as well and not just pass in my subjects. I wanted to ace them even if it seemed like an impossible thought at times. I pushed myself to the point where I deemed it impossible before even starting. My grades had started getting better, and I had hope of raising them from a 0.4 Gpa. However, the faith people had in me motivated me to work harder. I was not doing this to satisfy anyone else, and my achievements would benefit no one except for me. I took a while to understand that, but I somehow made it into Village Academy High school.

This placed proved to be the best thing for me. Coach Rob had done so much for me in this life, and he requested me something that would help me academically move forward. When I was working hard to raise my grades, sometimes I wanted to give up. I wanted to give up on this whole idea and live my life as it was. I later realized that I was wasting away my life by hanging out with people who would not matter in the next five years. However, I would waste away my five years having no academic achievement. But after getting admission at the village academy high school, I was glad I did not give up on myself. Village Academy felt like a second home.

As soon as I entered Village Academy, every student instantly fell in love with me. I'm not saying this to pull my leg, but most of the girls came up to talk. Perhaps it was my athletic figure that attracted them towards me, but I knew that they did not hate me in this place. I felt more comfortable here. To this day, I cannot bring myself to forget how everyone at the Village Academy liked me easily. Most of the teachers, not all, loved me despite my attitude. I never misbehaved for no reason, so that was something they liked about me. The change in the environment shifted something inside of me, and I felt motivated, as well. I told myself that I could do anything I could ever want if I put my mind to it, and I put my mind in playing football. Football was more than just a sport for me.

It was an activity where I could convey my true feelings. The rush and thrill that came with playing football were more elevating than getting drunk and high in bad company. I wanted to see myself standing in the middle of the stadium with roaring cheers from the audience. I wanted to see the blinding lights of the stadium shining down at me, and I wanted to be the star of the sport. I played football whenever I could find myself some time. I played many positions while I played games in the village academy such as the runner-back, kick-return, kickoff, defense of line, mostly every position applicable in football.

There was not a single position that I was terrible at. Because of my athletic abilities, every one of my team members loved me and relied on me heavily. I was not the only good player in the field, though, but the coaches always told me I was exceptionally good. Everything in my life seemed to revolve around football, and I spent most of my free time playing football.

I placed my focus entirely on the football practices that would take place with the team. Doing so helped me in staying out of the streets. I no longer felt thrilled by the life that the streets displayed, and I thought I had learned my lesson well enough at that point. Smoking weed or drinking alcohol would not help me improve my life, and discovering my dedication to football helped me stay out of trouble. As time passed in the Village Academy, I started involving myself with the right crowd.

I stopped going down the wrong path, and everything seemed to go well. I passed Fcat in 11th grade, which at one point, had seemed like a hurdle for me. However, I had somehow passed all my classes in just one go. I could not believe it, but I was improving academically and mentally. The environment we surround ourselves has a direct effect on our behaviors. The moment I had stepped into Juve, I had felt like the worst criminal on this earth. But being placed into Village Academy felt like I was being given a second chance in my life.

I thought I was doing whatever I could in my power not to ruin this chance, but I was far from improving myself in other parts. I still had a bad attitude, and I did not know how to get over that. Perhaps the experiences had beaten the wrong attitude in me, but I could not get out of it. I had always been impulsive, even as a child. I always acted first and thought about it later. Most people would think first, then act on their intentions, but I mostly just did whatever I wanted to do. I had no care in this world and cared about nothing but playing football.

I was a good player, but that was only in the fields. Just because I was a good player, did not immediately make me a good person. I had yet to understand what it takes to be good, from inside out. However, being surrounded by four walls of a classroom always suffocated me. The thought of sitting and doing nothing seemed pointless after going through an immense struggle of raising my GPA. Falling into old habits was an addicting process, and like an addict, I would always get back into the same old habits.

I was still a bad student in the books of some of my teachers. It was mainly because I would disturb the class daily. I would always talk back to the teachers or get into an argument with another student during the class sessions. My teachers would always tell me I was disrupting their class, but I never behaved apologetically. Life had yet to teach me how to get a good attitude. The complaints kept on piling up, and eventually, I ended up getting sent to the office because filing a complaint against me was not enough to help me gain sense. I always wondered if I did this to myself on purpose.

I would find a good path for myself and then wander off it within the next few months. I sat in the principal's office, and like any other teenager, I was unconcerned with my behavior with teachers. One of my football coaches was present during the time they sent me to the principal's office, and he told me something that angered me immediately. *"If you get in trouble in class, you don't get to play."*

I exploded on him and told him it was unfair of him to do something like this. I could not just stop playing football because of this. It made little sense, and at some point thought they were unfair to me. I got into a massive argument with my coach and told them that I would quit if they did something like this. Maybe I did not like the hold they had over me because they knew how important football was for me.

Or perhaps because I would taste the consequences of yet another action. After my anger calmed down, I sat down and thought about it deeply. I wondered if it was possible for me to give up on football when my team members relied on me. Working in a team is being a part of a unit. With a unit missing, the entire team cannot function properly. I thought about how I would let my team members down if I gave up on football right now. Thinking deeply about my mistakes helped me realize that I needed to own up and correct my mistakes. I finally apologized to my coach and my team members. I did not want to let them down because of the trust and faith they had in me.

All of us ended up going home after I apologized to them a few days later, and finally, in my junior year, I ended up playing the next game, but I had to clean up the field after practice every day until my coach told me I don't need to do it anymore. Life has a strange way to knock us down over and over again. Perhaps life is meant to be filled with challenges that would motivate us to move ahead or help us stay focused on our goals regardless of what we would face. Perhaps it was meant to knock us down to humble us. I did not know for sure. I just knew that life was meant to be lived while facing these challenges head-on. I faced yet another difficult problem in the next chapter of my life, and for the first time, I was unsure if I could come out unscathed.

I carried a lot of scars with myself, and this new incident was going to be the worst part of my life. That is saying something because I had already gone through so much in a short span of my life. Becoming a senior came with challenges of its own, and to my surprise, those challenges were not related to my academic performances.

Instead, all the hurdles I faced were related to yet another death of a person I held dear and close to my heart. One would think living through the death of my father would prepare me for the future. But I was far from being ready. I learned through life that no matter how many deaths you see around you, nothing in this world can ever prepare you for the aftermath.

MATTHEW B. HOLLAND

Chapter 9
How I Prove Everybody Wrong About Me

We all truly loved my cousin, and there will always be a part of me that would feel like I had let him down. I cannot help but think of the 'what if's' whenever I think about him. What if I had been the one with him that night instead of my brother, Willie? Would things had been any different? Or would I end up as Willie with two bullet wounds embedded into my skin as a constant reminder of what took place night?

A part of me wants to know what it would have or could have, been like if only I were there. But wondering about these things became pointless at some point. I knew Davon also loved us back, and that matters the most. All of us loved him, and he loved us back. That's who Davon, and that is who he will be for the rest of my life. The deaths of my father and cousin affected me the most, but there was a particular moment in my childhood that completely changed me forever.

I am unsure whether that change is good or not to this very day. There are times when I get some time to think about my life correctly, and I somehow end up thinking about DC and Rock as well. They were a good part of my life and only left bitter memories in their wake for me to remember. They changed me, and perhaps that change took place so that I could protect myself from feeling more pain in my life. I had already gone through so much in my life, but there was something particularly painful that had happened in my childhood. It was a different kind of pain, and it left a different sort of ache behind. Family can be the strongest team on the earth and also the most fragile bunch at the same time. All it takes is miscommunication and misunderstanding to break family ties.

Everyone, at some point in life, has a falling out with a member of a family, but these fallouts can always be repaired by talking out. I strayed from the wrong path, and it was addicting enough to make me fall into the right path again. The first time I stirred trouble as a child, my father scolded me for it. The second time I stirred trouble in my life, he was no longer there to scold me. I think that is why I acted out in the first place. Losing father took its toll on every one of us. My siblings and I felt lost in the world. My mother, although she did not show it, I know she must have felt all alone.

Our family broke down into individuals. Every one of us went out to explore ourselves, and due to the lack of supervision, I ventured down the wrong path. The choices were mine at the end of the day. I cannot place the blame on anyone but myself. The bitter part of me wanted to find something to place the blame on, but I was no longer a child and so could not keep on misplacing the blame.

Entering the juvenile jail knocked that sense into me, and I had to learn how to walk again after falling down on the dark path. That period of my life was the toughest. I had to sit and think about the life choices I made - befriending the wrong people, as well as going along with their whims for the sake of the thrill. The difficult aspect was coming to terms with my own demons and challenging them head-on. Have you ever confronted your flaws and thought of numerous ways to improve them? That is what I had to go through. I had to seek a way to improvise the flawed parts of myself before I ended up destroying my future.

My mother stuck by me. She was my greatest support system during the toughest period of my life. Every parent feels a sense of obligation to provide everything for their children, but everything she provided me with was out of a sense of love. She always made sure I had everything I needed in my life.

I had the best clothes and shoes despite the circumstances I lived in. It was all thanks to her. She stayed with me throughout the entire journey of coming to terms with myself. Where most parents would give up on their child who commits an armed robbery, she encouraged me to work harder to become a better person in my life. As a parent, she rectified my mistakes and told me right from wrong. There was this one time when I talked back to my teacher when I was in high school.

My mother confronted me on that and asked me, *"Why did you talk back to your teacher?"*

"I was having a bad day, ma." I told her, *"The teacher was pushing my buttons today. She was trying to rile me up."*

"Whatever the reason may be, you will not talk back to your teachers again. Am I understood, young man?" She asked me in a stern voice, and I nodded obediently.

"Yes, ma'am."

After that, my mother made sure I always stayed out of trouble and scolded me whenever I did something wrong. She was my backbone. I stayed out of trouble, given how she positively influenced me. She wanted me to improve for myself. She did not want me to improve for her sake or anyone else. She had told me that I had to be the one to save myself from there.

After putting on the best behavior, I was released from the county jail. I was given another opportunity to improve my life and myself, but I had yet to learn my lesson properly. I had reached 9th grade but had not improved myself. I did not commit any extreme crimes or threaten anyone's safety but my own. I hung out with the wrong crowd until everything came crashing down along with my education and

GPA. The entire situation was hopeless. When I told my coach Rob about my problem, he sought a solution for me. He gave me the goal of entering the Village Academy. But there was a catch. To join the academy, I had to raise my GPA. After working the entire summers away to improve my grade, I somehow ended up with a more than average GPA. I had improved, and my life was going good. I was trying to improve and doing well. My life had been perfect, my grades were perfect, and my games were going well.

My dream of becoming a professional football player had been alive until another tragedy stuck around in my life. The death of my cousin, Davon, left me with a different kind of ache in my heart. Where my father's death had led me to act out, my cousin's death led me to keep improving myself over and over again. Every time I felt like giving up, the thought of living a life that would go to waste always messed me up in my head. Davon did not get an opportunity to live his life to the fullest, and because of that, his life felt like a waste to him. His death motivated me to become something in this world — someone who will be worthy of being remembered. So I shifted my focus from the football games and placed it on my studies.

I studied harder than ever and somehow managed to graduate high school with a 2.4 GPA. The day of my graduation was one of the precious days of my life. I look back on that day with an elated feeling in my chest, telling me to keep moving forward in this life. We all go through several graduations, but it was the one day in my life when I felt as if I had accomplished a lot in my life. I carried valuable lessons with myself on that day. Prior to the graduation day, the principal of the Village Academy expressed that he wanted to mention my name in his speech that day.

"Can I use you as a reference in my speech?" The principal asked me a day before graduation.

I was bewildered with his request and asked him, *"You really want to use my name in your speech? Mine?"* I asked him to confirm.

"Yes," he replied, and so I agreed to it.

I was more of a *go with the flow* kind of guy, and there was no harm in him using my name in his speech on the most important day of my life. The graduation day was special, and but not every one of my family members came to my graduation day. There was just my mother, my cousin Robert, my other cousin Sharemah, and Davon's mom BJ.

His parents had a big argument with my mom and my siblings due to his untimely death, but despite having a fallout with us, his mom came to see me on my big day. They came around after making amends. That is the true power of the family. We all unite to share happiness and sadness. As the graduation processed, the school principal gave a short speech that I will remember for as long as I live.

He had gotten up on the stage and said, *"One day, I was walking down the hallway and met a student. His name was Matthew Holland. He had recently lost his cousin in a crossfire. I walked up to him and asked if he was going to get the boys back for doing that to his cousin. The boy looked at me and said, 'Sir, I want to be somebody in my life. I want to accomplish great things in my life, and ending up in prison is not one of them.'"* I could tell he was proud of me for graduating. He knew I was the first one in my family to graduate high school. As soon as he finished his speech, the entire auditorium erupted in cheers. I looked around. Every single person present at graduation was clapping for me. They were cheering on, just for me. I was taken back by surprise because I did not think I had done something to be cheered on. All I was trying to do was do justice with my life and be good.

I was trying to stay out of trouble, and now here I was, walking down the stage to take my hard-earned diploma. It was not only a diploma for me. It was all of my efforts and hard work. It was something I had attained after working day and night. The best part was knowing that I had attained it with my head held high. Mostly, it was through my own help that I came to this point in my life where I could be proud of something. The entire audience stood up and clapped for me when my name was called out.

Another chapter of my life came to an end, and I finally graduated high school. Graduating must not be a big deal for everyone, but for me, it was a big deal. I had accomplished a milestone in my life, something I thought I would never be capable enough to do in my life. Doing something like this was the last thing on my mind. The fact that I pushed myself past my limits to accomplish graduation in my life was like a dream come true. Everyone wanted to take pictures with me on that day because the principal had specifically taken my name. I thought, *oh damn, I'm already famous*. It was the best feeling in the world, and I was happy while it lasted.

After graduating from high school, I got into college. Life had taught me better, and I did not let this opportunity go to waste. I got into college, passed all my courses, and made the best out of my life. People believe that opportunities are only given to those who are privileged, but that is what the world wants them to believe in. There was no way an underprivileged child like me could have made it this far in my life. We all deserve to make our place in this world. None of us has to stick by the mistakes we make in our past. There is a reason why we should leave our past behind. Hanging onto the past only prevents us from moving forward in our life. When we stop moving forward in our life, we forever remain stranded in the middle of our journey. We wander toward all the right places, and this puts our progress on hold.

Everyone in my life always supported me and picked me up whenever I fell down. They always pushed me to look forward instead of looking back. How can someone move forward if they are not willing to make any progress in life? Our entire life depends on making progress along the way. Improving yourself is an ever-going process. If you run away from the idea of improving yourself, then you are the only one who is holding yourself back.

It is a continuous process that never comes to a stop until the day we die. There are many mistakes we make along our way. If we refuse to learn from these mistakes and keep repeating them, then we are walking down the road of self-destruction. To live is to errors. All of us will keep making human errors as we keep taking one step after another. But making errors is just a part of living our lives, and the best way to overcome this is to make sure that you learn a lesson from these errors so that you never repeat them. Life is unpredictable, but there is nothing we can do about its unpredictability.

Maybe it is a blessing that life is unpredictable because if we were able to predict our life, then we would live in a constant state of fear with the possibilities that would take place. I am a firm believer that everything happens for a reason, which is beyond our comprehension. As humans, we can never really make sense out of this life even if we try hard. I never tried to figure out my life until I had to sort it out. That was when I realized that there was no reason to make sense out of this life I had, but I had to make the most out of it.

My experiences shaped me into who I was and helped me walk down the path of self-improvement instead of pondering on my misfortunes. I learned the hard way that pitying yourself would only turn our living into a walking nightmare. The moment a person gives up on themselves is the moment when they are bound to kill themselves on the inside over and over again. The moment they give up on hope is the moment when they are truly abandoning themselves. No one can save you if you do not want to be saved. When you give up on yourself is the moment when you decide that nothing is worthy of living. Life becomes pointless and meaningless. Falling into the depth of despair will not do anything but harm your pride and sense of self. Nothing in this life can be worse than losing the sense of self, because that is the moment you become a nomad in this world.

You venture into territories you never ventured, and the journey might be exciting. The excitement is fleeting, and the pleasure gained out of the senseless wandering ends with a jolt. At some point, this only pulls you down until it is too late to pick yourself up. The moment you feel like falling off the edge is the moment you should pull yourself back before taking a dive. That does not mean that you grow up to be cautious of everything going on around you, but it does not hurt to be a little safe than sorry.

Our entire life hinges on the decisions we make in this world. Every choice we make has a consequence. It is not necessary for the consequences to show up right after we make a choice. Those consequences can show up days, weeks, months, or years later. That is how unpredictable our life is. The choices of our today hold the potential of destroying our future if we end up making a wrong one in continue to make the wrong decisions. However, the right choices we make in this life can set up our entire future.

We should all learn how to live our life while maintaining a balance in this world. It is not possible not to make the wrong choices, but there is always the possibility of improving ourselves by learning from the choices we have made. Living in the past holds you back, and living in the future makes you stop living in the moment.

There should be a fine balance between these worlds. It is imperative to learn from the past and grow in the present to improve our future. My life only ended up being good because I had decided to make it good. I had all the wrong choices laid in front of me, and I chose those paths because I was unaware of all the good choices that I should have taken. There were moments when I thought it was too late to improve myself.

It was a mantra in my head that went like, *"It's too late to make amends. It's too late to improve myself and my life."*

But there was a voice at the back of my head that told me to keep pushing forward.

"So what if it's too late? What's the harm in trying? It's not like I'm going to end up losing something. I'm only going to gain more in life if I try."

And so I pushed myself. I lived through my life. There were moments when I laughed and rejoiced in my life. Then there were the dark periods in my life when I lost my father and went ahead in my life only to lose one of my beloved cousins who was closer to my age.

After going through so many trials in my life, I had finally graduated and learned to move forward in my life. Life is a series of misfortunes waiting to happen, but it is also a series of unforgettable events. The only thing we can do is savor the moment and make decisions in our life carefully to avoid facing problems in the future. None of us is given a good or a bad life. It all depends on us whether we want to make a good life or a bad one.

All it takes is dedication and resilience to make it this far in life. I walked down this path of life as a boy, only to come out as a man after going through trials and tribulations sent my way. My life was all about becoming a man in a tough journey. I would not have it any other way. Experiences shaped me into a better man. All it took was patience to help me reach this point of elevation in my life, and nothing more. After graduating from high school, I got into Edward Waters college College on a football scholarship. I was really excited because I never thought I would ever get far enough in life to get enrolled in a college.

Every single member of my family hardly made it to high school graduation, but here I was, the first one in the family to get into college. The moment I walked onto a college campus on my first day, everything felt surreal. Edward Waters College was one of the oldest colleges in Florida. Everyone in my family supported me tremendously - even one of my older cousins, Al, who also lived in Jacksonville, Florida. He was so excited to see me in college that he always provided me with food and little things like hygiene deodorant etc. to make sure I was doing well. He made sure that I was doing good at college and concentrated on my studies. I passed through the freshman year and acquired a GPA of 3.5 smoothly. I was really focused, and I also ended up making great friends. They were Ocean and Kernard. They made me laugh for real and were a lot of fun.

My GPA started to drop a little bit in my sophomore year in college. It was not bad, but it was not good either. But I was hurting a lot that year; I got a call one night that said my brother Jarvis had gotten shot. All I could think was how I wouldn't get to see my brother ever again. I used to stay the nights at his house, and his family loved me as well. In my junior year in college, I had joined a fraternity called Phi Beta Sigma. It was the best thing that had ever happened to me because I made a lot of brothers during that time. I had five brothers who came out with me.

The first one was Dj, the second was Kp, the third was Jay, and then came Sam and Curt. They all came out with me and hung out with me every day. They were great brothers and always had my back. We had meetings together to make the community better. They were one of the few people who supported me at all times. Besides them, my college teachers also supported me as they had seen how my grades had fallen during my junior year. Among the people who supported me, the people who supported me the most were Mrs. Matthews, Dr. Conley, and Mrs. Richardson. Mrs. Lipede was my second mom, and also Mrs. Summers. The year was a crazy one as my close friend, Greg Bryant, was also shot in the head back in my hometown. I could not believe it. This man was on his way to the NFL. I guess the good die. Everything changed during my senior year. I worked and handled a job, along with my studies. I worked for this man named Richard - me and my cousin Courtney. My cousin was the one who helped me get the job. I ended up staying with him throughout my senior year in college, as I didn't have enough money to pay for my room.

He and his girlfriend Jass helped me out a lot, so I could graduate college. I'm really thankful to them. My cousin Courtney and I worked as lumberjacks; we used to cut the wood. I would chop it up into pieces, and it would be delivered to the food company. I only worked as a lumberjack on the side. I was juggling an internship I had gotten at the YMCA, and there I met some great people. I was a part of a nonprofit organization that worked with the kids as well. I did a lot of things during my senior year.

When I made it to graduation, Coach Rob came as well as all of my teachers from high school. My entire family was there because I was the first person who reached college graduation in my family. My mom cried a lot, but I knew she was crying out of happiness. I always wanted to make something out of my life, and without realizing it, I became someone who knew what to do in life. It meant a lot to me, and I wanted to pass on the message to other kids like me back in my hometown. I want them to realize that it does not matter where you come from, but the only thing that matters in life is where you are trying to go in life. I always pushed myself to become the best person I could be as a man, and I always wanted to make my mother proud. College helped me grow into the man that I am today. I achieved everything in life due to the mindset I have, and that allowed me to push harder. Life had taught me better, and I did not let this opportunity go to waste. I got into college, passed all my courses, and made the best out of my life.

Everyone in my life always supported me and picked me up whenever I fell. They always pushed me to look forward instead of looking back at my life. How can someone move forward if they are not willing to make any progress in life? Our entire life depends on making progress along the way. Improving yourself is an ever-going process. If you run away from the idea of improving yourself, then you are the only one holding yourself back.

TO BE CONTINUED... MOVE TO TEXAS!!!!

Made in the USA
Columbia, SC
14 April 2021